Beneath the Canopy

Michelle Cook

Copyright © 2018 Michelle Cook

All rights reserved.

ISBN-10: 1948469006
ISBN-13: 978-1948469005

DEDICATION

For you…

Beneath the Canopy

Mature swaying branches
Hover serenely above
Creating a secluded place
To share our enduring love

Billowy white clouds
Float leisurely overhead
Taking us to places
Which we cannot comprehend

A contented sigh escapes
As we linger awhile longer
The pleasant summer breeze
Leaves our minds to wander

Memories of simpler times
Preoccupy our thoughts
Such remembrances appearing
As blurry snapshots

As twilight descends around us
We know we must say farewell
Yet the lovely canvas in front us
Has cast its magical spell

We further delay our departure
For one final passionate kiss
As moments like these are scarce
And must not be dismissed

At last needing to part ways
We lovingly say goodbye
Leaving behind one another
With impossible tears in our eyes

Somehow we both know
That we will never again see
This beautiful rare scene
Beneath the canopy

Timeless Love

Excitement builds
As you wait for the day
To see your old friend
On an arranged holiday

As the day draws near
You become quite giddy
You plan to meet each other
In a faraway city

Questions cross your mind
And you're apprehensive
You can only wonder
If she'll find you offensive

When the day finally comes
A strange pit forms in your gut
You know you must play it safe
No matter what

Shaking in your boots
You pray she still finds you attractive
Considering your age
You hope she'll be adaptive

Stepping off the plane
You see her slender form
She smiles and waves at you
From the small open door

More questions flood your mind
About what she'll think
Will she still want you
Or will this be a huge mistake

You clutch the flowers tighter
A bouquet bought just for her
She begins to run to you
And all becomes a blur

Tears quickly emerge
You've captured her awaiting heart
Instantly you wonder
How you ever made it apart

Clutching one another
As if your life depends on this embrace
You both feel emotions
Which cannot be erased

Neither one of you
Can hold back the steady stream of tears
The warmth of her body
Erases all your fears

Finally you know for certain
She's always been the one
You eagerly kiss her lips
And look forward to some fun

She reciprocates your affections
And smiles in satisfaction
Nothing can thwart
This overwhelming attraction

It's been many long years
Yet somehow love remained
You realize now
Your love was not in vain

Us

There's chemistry between us
A fire that can't be quenched
Something quite unexpected
Easily takes away my breath

Spiritually connected as well
Tied together when we're apart
Can't understand its meaning
Draws my mind right to your heart

Joined together by true friendship
A rare occurrence for days we live
Blessed by your heartfelt presence
In a world which doesn't easily give

The depth of my despair evaporates
Your warm existence takes it away
Scars of a painful and bitter past
Simply removed by what you say

Shall We?

Yes I admit
I'm a hopeless dreamer
A fun-loving
Fantasy seeker
Living for
The rare occasion
To share more
Than a conversation
Enticing words
Can be highly effective
It all depends
On the receiver's perspective
So without
Further elaboration
Care to join me
In this collaboration?

Magnetic

The waves pummeled and crushed
The shimmery glittering sand
As he longingly reached out
For her exquisitely formed hand

An unrelenting powerful attraction
Between the two of them grew
And like strong compelling magnets
They both now finally knew

It was futile for either of them
To resist the alluring urge
As their flirtatious wanton bodies
Couldn't help but begin to merge

Suddenly the blooming horizon
Reacted with a rosy blush
As the two lovers moved closer
Lost in each other's sultry touch

The day expeditiously ended
With one lasting passionate kiss
One which evoked feelings
Of impassioned and euphoric bliss

And secret eternal wishes
Were silently and enduringly made
As amorous thoughts of affection
Were completely and abundantly displayed

Thinking of You…

Thoughts of you
Cross my mind
As the water rushes
Down my spine

Imagining your touch
Our bodies interlaced
Parts of me
Your tongue would taste

Chills and tingles
Run straight through
Caressing myself
The way you would do

Envisioning your body
Pressed against mine
Sliding your fingers
Deeper inside

The shower drowns out
My screams of pleasure
This fantasy of you
Just keeps getting better

Lost Love

There was never a goodbye
Just empty words which made her cry
There was never a farewell
Just broken promises which left her unwell
There was never a final note
Just remembrances of things he wrote
There was never a happy ending
Just the blessing of a brand new beginning

Making a Memory

I made a lasting memory
Of your face today
As you sat on the bed
You happened to glance my way

Your eyes then stared back
Gazing into mine
Capturing that fleeting moment
Almost lost in a second of time

Never will I forget
The look upon your face
The meaning behind your smile
Will never be erased

Entangled thoughts lingered
In the space in-between
And you stole my longing heart
In a moment I hadn't foreseen

Borrowed Heart

I borrowed your heart for a day
I desperately needed the time away
And although there wasn't much to say
You listened and cried with me anyway
Now I can only hope and pray
That eventually I will find my way
Thanks for lending your heart for a day

Michelle Cook

The Very Idea of You

The very idea of you
Makes my heart race
The words you've spoken
My mind cannot erase

A million creative sparks
Flow through my mind
Every time I imagine
You and I entwined

Your face is all I see
In the dark of the night
Escaping with you
In every word that I write

Longing for your touch
Envisioning you here
Praying to God
That you never disappear

You're the only one who rescues me
From my depressive self
The only one who doesn't leave me
Alone on a dusty shelf

Beneath the Canopy

You inspire my mind
As well as my body and soul
You're the only one who leaves me
Without any self-control

You keep me always wanting
So much more of you
And you're the only one around
Who can ever pull me through

What more can I say
It's you that I completely adore
Thoroughly smitten
And hoping for so much more

Michelle Cook

The Night They First Met

In the dingy dark room
They sat and they talked
The conversation was light
Their boring lives they forgot

An old faded yellow couch
Sank deeper with every word
Dreams and wishes were shared
And both were finally heard

All too soon the black of night
Faded into a brand new day
They both felt immensely pleased
By what the other had to say

It was an evening to remember
One they'll never be able to forget
As it was the best night of their lives
Since it was the night that they first met

Enticed

Enticed by his sweet lips
Her hesitations finally dissolved
And after one delicious taste
She was hopelessly involved

His luscious kisses convinced her
To give into her passionate desires
And from that day forth
She was forevermore inspired

Michelle Cook

Reminders of an Enduring Connection

Hundreds of letters
Were eagerly written
By a boy and a girl
Who were thoroughly smitten

Glitter filled envelopes
Often contained
A thousand sparkly hearts
Meant to entertain

A million thoughts were sealed
With enthusiastic kisses
Every hope and dream confessed
Exposed secretly shared wishes

Blossoming love adorned
The many tear-filled pages
As hearts began to overindulge
During various stages

Passion often waged war
On their tender hearts and minds
This sort of love mimicked
That of the permanent kind

After awhile they could no longer deny
An everlasting union
As they both knew this wasn't
Just some made-up illusion

Glittering hearts
Soon entwined
With a traditional toast
Of sparkling wine

And those captured words
Of affection
Still remain as reminders
Of their enduring connection

The Sweetest Kiss

The sweetest kiss ever
Was yours and yours alone
It brought me more happiness
Than I've ever really known

The gentle brush of your lips
Willed mine to agreeably part
Affectionately confiscating my mind
And fully capturing my longing heart

Intermingled

Intermingled within
The threads of time
Connectivity heightened
By riddles and rhyme
Thoughts and wonders
Bewilder and entice
Flooding the mind
With a cost and a price

A Love Like This

In his loving arms
I gently lay
Resting quietly
At the end of the day

He holds me close
Wipes a tear from my cheek
His infinite love
Is what I seek

A love like this
Is rare and true
Sought by many
Yet far and few

This love is more
Than worldly passion
Specially made
Designed and fashioned

A treasured gift
Created just for me
And it's only him
My heart can see

Summer Surrender

The moon alights the cloud barren sky
Ripples of sultry waters glide with ease
Lingering beneath her pale breasts

She inches tentatively forward
Approaching his awaiting arms
The desire in his eyes remains clear
His sensuous smirk is playfully inviting

A warm summer mist rises off the lake
The foggy vapor slightly obscures
The arousing chill upon her breasts

He reaches out beneath the cool waters
Capturing her delicate form
Drinking in her illuminated artistry
Memorizing every visible feature

Captivated by what she freely gives
He accepts her affections without hesitation
Reveling in what she lovingly surrenders

Michelle Cook

The Old Married Couple

Basking in the glow
Of a warm winter fire
He looks at her
With his usual nervous desire

She soon takes notice
Of his common timid nature
And tries to ease
His typical introverted behavior

Playful shy glances
Send out invisible sparks
An illuminating display
Of unspoken wishes in the dark

Daring to be the one
To make the first move
She subtly slides over
Beaming as he approves

Nestled in the embrace
Of an enduring love
They fit together
Like an old familiar glove

Happy and content
Just to sit and snuggle
Yes this is the life
Of an old married couple

You Exist

I see you
In the rushing waters
Of the glittering
Sun kissed waves

As they leap happily
Upon the shore
Lingering briefly
Where you once stood

I hear you
In the gentle rustle
Of the vibrant
Autumn leaves

Each one
Shivers excitedly
In anticipation
Of your loving touch

I feel you
In the wisps
Of the cool
Embracing winds

Beneath the Canopy

As they tenderly
Caress my skin
Reminding me
That you are near

Overcome by Desire

Instantaneous fire
Set fully ablaze
As his longing eyes
Meet her eager gaze

Both entranced
By visions of passion
Words not needed
In this magnetic reaction

Suspense gathers
Neither looking away
Surging feelings
Enticing each to stay

Desires embraced
By fateful attraction
Empowered by love
Both take action

The course is set
Any doubts erased
Moving toward one another
Both hearts race

Beneath the Canopy

Finally engaging
Nervous hands merge
Intoxicating excitement
Both feel the surge

Delirious fascination
Envelopes each soul
Each quite certain
Of losing all control

Joined by forces
Neither one can see
Only time will tell
If they are meant to be

Waves of Emotions

My emotions surge
From one day
To the next
My mind
Races frequently
And is often
Perplexed

I've watched sweet chivalry
Come unexpectedly
Then go
Witnessed
A wave of emotions
Swaying haphazardly
To and fro

Some days are exciting
Others
Boring and bland
Electricity
Fires up
At the touch
Of his warm hand

Exploring every option
As he
Explores his own
Hoping In the end
For a place
We'll both
Call home

Seduced

Her silence was interrupted
By the touch of his lips
And he smothered her mouth
With a warm luscious kiss

A sudden crushing embrace
Left her head spinning
Leaving her speechless
And inwardly grinning

Hands began frantically
To grab and tear clothes
This sudden turn of events
Left her quite literally exposed

Consumed by desire
For his sudden affections
She succumbed to his needs
Without any objections

Irresistible Words

Charming words danced around her head like raindrops in slow motion
The breeze collected her thoughts and suspended them in mid-air
Time stood still in those surreal moments and blooming hearts entwined
Distance could not break the surge of electricity that permeated
Neither the vast sea nor the highest mountain could freeze the pull
Bound by dreams and visions and enraptured by similar ambition
The intense response was undeniably authentic and captivating
The utterance of words so elementary and yet so unbelievably profound
Heartfelt declarations sealed their eternal fate and love blossomed

Love in the Midst of Uncertainty

Unexpectedly bewitched
And profoundly mystified
Each become enthusiastically
Obsessed one to the other
Overwhelming passion
Leads to spellbound senses
Magnetic forces accelerate
The compelling connection
Perceptive thoughts thoroughly
Examine the situation
Both seek complete understanding
And clarification
She discerns his character
While he studies her nature
He senses her expectant desires
While she fully recognizes his
At last settled minds
Arouse captivated hearts to eagerly advance
Every questionable thought
Is now completely abandoned
Impetuous emotions commence
While provocative words hover playfully
Finally reacting as tousled raindrops
Fluctuate invitingly over an alluring current
Destiny is set into motion
And love is captured in the midst of uncertainty

Him…

Reaching out
Both know what they're after
His mouth brushes lightly against hers
The sensation heightens their emotions
Each knows this is what they've been missing
Hands move to embrace one another
Bodies melding into one
Hearts on fire
Shaking in anticipation for what is to come
Their kisses go deeper
Igniting senses that were never felt before
Pulling closer
They cannot get close enough
Hands begin to maneuver their way down
Seeking the warmth of flesh
Aching to be touched
His hands find pleasure
In the warmth of her breasts
Another glance into the window of her soul
Then kisses glide down her body
Tickling her flesh
Causing emotions to soar even higher
His mouth finds one of her blushing nipples
And he teases it gently with his tongue
The hardness of him aches to be released
And she reaches down to explore him

Stroking him gently at first
Then with greater intensity
He moves one of his hands to find her secret place
She urges him closer
Clothing completely shed
Each is ready to feel what a lifetime away
Has kept them from
Entering her slowly at first
The sensation sends electrifying shocks of ecstasy
Coursing through her body
The power of emotion in this moment
Surges like never before
She begs him to enter her further
Wanting him fully inside
He takes what she offers
Feeling the wetness of her core
Against his own hard erection
Penetrating her deeper
Until he can barely keep from losing all control
The intensity grows
And he feels her tighten against his hard shaft
Every thrust sends out sensations which beg for more
Neither wanting to end this pleasurable experience
Each holds on tighter
Fighting the urge for release
Begging the sensations to last
Slowing to allow their bodies to settle
Not wanting this moment to end

Beneath the Canopy

The warmth and intensity
Of what is finally taking place
Overwhelms them
And they begin again
Going even deeper this time
Moving together as one
At last neither can hold back any longer
The need is too great
And both seek
What they have forever been longing for
At last sweltering bodies give themselves up
Waves of ecstasy wash over
Leaving lasting impressions
Feelings once denied have finally been revealed
And hearts unite as one

Destined

Her dress was made of cotton
And smelt of sweet perfume
And her heavenly scent enticed him
On that endearing afternoon

An unfaltering gaze between them
Said everything they couldn't say
And they laid there with hands clasped
On that bright blue summer day

His smile caused a flutter
And her heart began to soar
Convinced of his love
She wanted to keep him forevermore

Her expression amused him
And her affections gripped his soul
She was the only woman alive
Who had ever made him feel whole

Their connection was unmistakable
They seemed destined from the very start
So they dreamt of a future together
Where nothing would ever keep them apart

The Heart String

An invisible string connects us
And no matter how far away you go
When I feel the gentle pull of the string
I'm instantly all aglow

I feel this gentle tug so often
And yet I never get tired of its hold
The string reminds me that you are always there
And will be until I'm quite old

Every day I think of you
Until the day is done
This string which ties us is completely unbreakable
And binds our hearts as one

So when you feel the pull
Of my devoted and warm loving soul
Don't forget that I am always here
Perpetually wishing you were near

Michelle Cook

Waves of Ecstasy

Crystal clear waters
Warm and enticing
The ocean's current
Serene and inviting

Turquoise blue sea foam
Drifts lazily along the shore
As enthralled young lovers
Undress and explore

The sea beckons softly
And before very long
The happy young couple
Slips into the beyond

Sliding beneath
The temperate swells
Each transfixed
By the other's hypnotic spell

Now fully overcome
With passion and desire
Discovering a love
Which will never expire

Beneath the Canopy

Moving closer together
On the uprising of the tide
She takes him fully
As he slips deep inside

Ecstasy now shown
Upon his charming face
Completely satisfied
In her amorous embrace

Mesmerized by each other
Lost in a dream all their own
Pleased by this rare moment
To be free and all alone

Amorous Afternoon

Fresh clean linen
On ivory smooth skin
Upon her face
An amusing grin

A single white rose
Flawless in form
The only thing
Which she adorns

Scent of gardenia
Lingers in the air
Petals now embellishing
Her long auburn hair

Beauty of light
She blushes for him
Instinctively satisfying
His every whim

Pure sweet blessedness
Fills the room
In the quiet hush
Of the amorous afternoon

The Old Porch Swing

Late in the evening
On the old porch swing
After the fireflies glow
And the crickets sing
It's just you and me
Left to the night
Smitten with each other
Under the stars so bright
Rocking back and forth
On the old porch swing
Trembling from the night air
And the shivers it brings
Nestling closer
Within your loving arms
Noticing your smile
And all your boyish charms
Enjoying every minute
Of our time together
During moments like these
I see our forever

You Are My Treasure

You are a rare gift that I treasure more with every passing day
Sometimes I trip and fall over the words that you say
Some days I can hardly believe how close I feel to you
And then other days I am left wondering if what you say is true
I have never felt this way about anyone before
You are the only one that I have ever truly adored
Like an angel looking out for me you came along
And when I think of you I am reminded of my favorite song
The way you've treated me has always been with utmost respect
And because of this we've been able to completely connect
I will forever cherish the love that you have shown to me
Beloved you are my treasure and always will be

Lazy Days

Goosebumps tingle
My satiny skin
Giggling as you
Gather me in
Soft caresses
As we embrace
Against cotton sheets
And silky black lace
Our bodies meld
And unite as one
As we disregard
The fast rising sun
Enjoying each other
In every possible way
Welcoming in
Another lazy day

Michelle Cook

It Had To Be You

All my life
I searched for you
Then one day
My dream came true

I saw you from across
A crowded room
Little did I know
We'd be married soon

The way you smiled
Made my heart skip a beat
I wondered for a moment
If I could even compete

Finally all doubt
Flew out the door
As I recognized it was you
I rather adored

I can't put into words
How I finally knew
Somehow I just realized
It had to be you

Enveloped in the Depths of Your Soul

Enveloped in the depths of your soul
I lose all rational thought and control

Yearning to stay in your arms forever
I can't get enough of you when we're together

My heart beats faster as you whisper in my ear
The only thing I want is to pull you nearer

My mind races and I can't catch my breath
Dying in your arms would be the perfect death

Michelle Cook

The Only One for Me

Kind eyes lure me in
Sweet chivalry works again
Honest words bring an everlasting trust
Heartfelt love is never about lust
You invade my thoughts with your boyish grin
Your sentimental charm reels me in
Thoughtful gifts leave me to wonder
Sensual thoughts pull me under
Knowing glances are just the beginning
Tender kisses set my head spinning
Your lingering touch awakens my soul
Your warm embrace makes me whole
Passionate cravings are just the start
Deep affection fills my heart
Alluring advances lead to unconstrained dances
At last fulfilled desires leave me giddy
Genuine approaches are never a pity
Gentle caresses slowly fade
As shared dreams eventually invade
Memories of enraptured delight
Sweep me into mornings light

A Lifetime Isn't Enough

Thoughts of you envelop
The depths of my abiding soul
A thousand words go unwritten
Merely waiting to be told
A lifetime isn't enough
To explain to you how I feel
Life is just all too short
For these pages to be filled

Michelle Cook

You've Captured My Heart

You captured my heart
Right from the start
I honestly don't know
How we've made it apart

You and I have
This crazy close connection
It's allowed me to make you
My one and only exception

Although I do wonder why
We have just met now
After each of us has already
Taken a lifelong vow

All day long
My mind wanders back to you
When I don't hear any word
I feel quite blue

I cherish every sentence
That you've ever written
With you I've certainly
Become quite smitten

Beneath the Canopy

Every time I think of you
My body feels strange
It's a weird sort of feeling
Which I can hardly explain

I want you to know
Exactly how I feel
I know this seems odd
Yet my feelings are real

I know you're already taken
Yet everything I say is true
And the only dream I have left
Is to someday be with you

Mediterranean Inspiration

Lying beside you
On the misty morning beach
Your inviting body
Is just within reach

Your smile is enticing
Encouraging me on
In your arms
Is where I belong

Quick to notice
Your playful eyes
Which now reflect
The coming sunrise

The crispness of
The newfound day
Mixes effectively
With the warm sea spray

Drawn to the warmth
Of your polished skin
Lifting the blankets
You gather me in

Beneath the Canopy

Clothing shed
Your body feels amazing
Your smoldering touch
Leaves me blazing

Lost in the moment
Kissing heightens the thrill
And the cool morning air
Now loses its chill

Intimately exploring
Your touch is divine
Under the covers
Our bodies align

Thoroughly enjoying
Every sensuous caress
Legs spread apart
Allowing full access

Hearts beat faster
As emotions rise
Your view now reflecting
The blue in my eyes

The present time escapes
Senses out of control
My heart and my mind
Forever lost in your soul

Inside Old Familiar Eyes

I saw a glimpse of you
Inside old familiar eyes
The intensity of your gaze
Such a wonderful surprise

You finally showed me
Who you really are
A stranger you had been
Even in my loving arms

I tried for years to find you
The way I knew I should
Yet closed off as you were
I never really could

Michelle Cook

How I See You

Your charm is delightful and brings joy to my heart
Your smile is contagious and won me from the start

Your body is perfect all rugged and strong
Your arms beg to comfort me when the day goes quite wrong

Your hands I presume to be warm and made for holding
Your touch I imagine as tender and never scolding

Your eyes invite passion and fill me with desire
Your gaze permeates my body and ignites a long lost fire

Your voice is a sound I hope one day to hear
Your presence is what I long to be near

Your poems speak of your loving affection
Your words spark our endearing connection

Your face is radiant and full of God's love
You are truly a gift sent from heaven above

Lost in His Kiss

Curling my toes
As I feel his lips
A heavenly feeling
Lost in his kiss

Gripping the sheets
As he begins to explore
Begging for mercy
From the one I adore

So Many Words

So many words
You've quietly said
Now swirl around
Inside my head

Beautiful words
Filled with hope
Keep me going
Help me cope

Loving words
Flood my heart
With the reassurance
Of a brand new start

Difficult words
Wisdom that hurts
Often feeling
Cold and curt

Secret words
Between you and me
Comfort my soul
And set me free

Dancing in the Clouds

Dancing under
A moonlit sky
Images of forever
Meander by

Loving caresses
Tease her skin
Capturing her heart
From deep within

Lost in his embrace
Away from the crowds
Feels like they're dancing
In the clouds

Pleasures of You

Dead of night
Your lips claimed mine
The taste was sweet
Like raspberry wine

Sensual kisses caressed
My delicate frame
Nipping and tugging
Fueling passionate flames

Our bodies were on fire
Steamy smoldering skin
Ripe and ready
Craving warmth deep within

Soaked silken sheets
Begged frantically for more
Unable to resist
We both proceeded to explore

Hardness at core
Felt throbbing in need
Consumed by lust
Filled with fiery greed

Beneath the Canopy

Pulling you closer
Willing you deeper inside
Taking you fully
Enjoying the ride

At last sated peak
Our body's glistened gold
Breath became even
More relaxed and controlled

Our limbs remained tangled
No beginning or end
Under mountains of muscles
You had me pinned

Lavishing the warmth
In an exhausted embrace
We both fell asleep
Fingers lovingly laced

This memory of you
I've kept close to my heart
I think I'd feel hopelessly lost
If we were ever to part

Michelle Cook

Imagining a Day with You

I'm sitting here trying to imagine
A day just with you

A day such as this
Would be a dream come true

So many endless possibilities
So many things we've missed

I keep trying to imagine
Our very first kiss

I wish with all my heart
We could eventually have this day

Holding each other tightly
We'd be completely swept away

I can imagine you lying next to me
With a contented look upon your face

Oh what I wouldn't give
For even just one warm embrace

Strangers

Two strangers became entranced
By the mere existence of the other

Both hopelessly plagued
By the inadequacies of their unfulfilled lives

When time happened along
And finally bestowed mercy by aligning their paths

His fingers trembled
At the thought of her very being

And she squirmed in anticipation
Of what his smoldering eyes revealed

Hearts exploded in a flood of emotions
As they finally embraced

And passion was finally born
In a world of broken dreams

The Enchanter

His hand held her throat
And she felt the rush of excitement
Cornered in a small alcove
She'd lured him by enticement

Finally he'd captured her
Amused by her playful banter
Moving his hands down to her waist
He'd now became the enchanter

His sweet seductive charm
Tempted her rational nature
And she stared at his handsome face
Memorizing every provocative feature

He began to tease her with delicate kisses
His hands pulling her closer and with haste
And any signs of potential hesitation
Were long forgotten as they fervidly embraced

Lovers Lane

Antique weathered lamp posts
Radiate their warm glowing hue
Each one casting inky shadows
Upon those unobservant few

There's a slight scent of rain
Hovering on the velvety breeze
While loves pure essence lingers
Amongst the silvery moonlit trees

Lovers stroll along the shadowy pathway
Each captivated by amorous thoughts
Lovingly sharing words of affection
And whispering forget-me-nots

Emotions surge as fingers are laced
Each one enthralled by the other
Never before have they felt this way
Except towards one another

My Love

I awake to your loving smile
A warmth brighter than the sun
Your smile is contagious
Your eyes so full of fun

You pull me in close
And our bodies meld together
I see only you my love
At last I've found my treasure

Rest in Me

Rest your head
Upon my chest
Soothing strokes
Always feel the best
Nestle within
The warmth of me
Open your heart
To what your eyes can't see

Pushing Through the Boundaries of Time

Pushing through
The boundaries of time
I rush right through and grab you
You're mine

Free at last
To have my way
Time completely stops
As we begin to play

Smiles abound
With carefree banter
You've always been the one
That I've been after

Pulling you close
Our clothing in disarray
Your body tells me
You want me to stay

This single moment in time
A rare sought after chance
To finally be with each other
And share some steamy romance

Beneath the Canopy

Your eyes are intent
And filled with hunger
My body is ready
As you pull me under

There's no hesitation
For what we're after
And my body responds
Wanting you deeper and faster

Your skin is hot
Against my flesh
The more I squirm
The harder you press

There's no stopping now
Completely engaged
Letting go of inhibitions
On this bare-skinned stage

You flood me with
Your life-giving vigor
And send me to a place
Of heavenly rigor

Pushing me to the edge
Of complete ecstasy
Responding to each one
Of my breathless pleas

There's no holding back
The surges of pleasure
The waves of release
Cannot be measured

Satisfied fully
We finally settle in
Bodies entwined
Still feeling you within

As the boundaries of time
Begin to close
We're at last swept away
In sweet contented repose

Images of You

Twilight comes
Thoughts of you invade
At the water's edge
Sadness begins to fade
For images of you
Dance through my mind
Music to my ears
Your sweet smile I find

Only Time Knows

You swept me away
To another place in time
As our lips embraced
And our bodies entwined

Your charm was intoxicating
My mind was a blur
You radiated confidence
And made my heart stir

Never in this life
Had I felt such bliss
Lost in the enchantment
Of your fiery kiss

If only these feelings
Could forever endure
And yet time is the only one
Who can completely assure

My One True Love

You're with me through my darkest days
Even during times when nobody else stays

You give me hope when I want to give up
There's nobody else who can measure up

You surround me with your daily presence
And remind me of your timeless acceptance

You bring to mind an extraordinary kind of love
Which only you can send from heaven above

You're all I need if truth be told
My one true love worth more than gold

Home

Your face I see clearly
Though you often try to hide
In your tear-filled eyes
Is where I permanently reside

It's the place we first met
So sad was the gaze
I reached out to touch you
And my mind was amazed

For how could I have found
A perfect mirror of me
Your stare so intense
Genuine love I could see

An ocean of warmth
Spread across me like fire
Your discerning familiar eyes
Fueled my passionate desire

And in that perfect moment
In a dream all our own
I finally knew for certain
What it was like to be home

The Day Truth Rained Down

She was bathed
In fragrant petals
As his luminous love
Rained down
Glimmering rays
Of flawless light
Began to sprinkle
Across the ground
She was flooded with
Profound wonder
As whispers of truth
Began to descend
And pristine streams
Of unblemished ecstasy
Vowed to carry her
To the triumphant end

You Were Made For Me

All of my senses
Are blissfully overpowered
As I breathe you in
Curled up beside you
I live for these moments
Endearing and passionate
Our hearts beat as one
Your strong fingers
Interlace my own
Hands designed specifically
With me in mind
This bond we share
Cannot be broken
Every intimate thought
Shared completely
Fully connected hearts
Souls entwined
I love you more
With every passing day
You were made for me
And I for you

Lost in the Hope of You

The world suddenly stopped
As we danced under a moonlight sky
Your look told me I was loved
There was no need to wonder why
We both felt the pull
As the earth began to spin
A flood of emotions were felt
From somewhere deep within
Tears fell from your eyes
As you looked down at me
Heartfelt intentions
I could finally see
Lost in all of our thoughts
Thinking back to days long past
We danced all night
Lost in the hope of romance

Michelle Cook

Realignment of a Broken Heart

Such a beautiful soul
Extremely willing and free
Eager to proclaim his love
As he got down on one knee

Yet her poor fragile heart
Remained broken apart
The pieces lay scattered
Like a crushed work of art

Though she tried to say yes
She was unable to speak
Though she knew that without him
Her life would be bleak

She sought inner strength
Which she carried deep within
And tried in earnest to explain
Not knowing where to begin

And as he held out his hand
Seeking the warmth of hers
His bright smile faded
As he listened to her words

Dismayed by the rejection
Of his one true love
He looked to the heavens
Seeking answers from above

And as his heartfelt pleas
For a response were sent
He sat there in anguish
With a look of regret

She quietly carried
Herself far away
Unsure of her actions
Her mind in complete disarray

She desperately wondered
If she had made the right choice
This really should have been
A day to rejoice

Still completely unsure
She desperately needed to know
Her heart had wanted to stay
Yet her head had told her to go

She stayed as far away as she could
Allowing time to pass by
Wondering why her choice
Seemed to only make her cry

The more she thought
The more confused she became
Until one day she found herself
Finally unable to abstain

She had to go back
To the love she had left
So very ill without him
She felt completely bereft

So eventually one day
She knocked on his door
Taken aback by her presence
He nearly landed on the floor

Tears filled his eyes
Waiting a lifetime for this day
It was what he had prayed for
The entire time she was away

Beneath the Canopy

He opened his arms wide
To embrace her unexpected return
His heart filled with tremendous relief
Realizing his love had not been spurned

Together they finally became one
Happier than most could ever be
It just took time and patience
For her heart and head to finally agree

Michelle Cook

Feeling Loved

As I laid there last summer
Under a brilliant blue sky
Friendships and love
Seemed to be passing me by

Many months slipped away
And I felt so alone
I just couldn't seem
To find a welcoming home

The Lord knew my heart though
And even when I hesitated to pray
He saw my urgent need for love
And answered me anyway

Little by little
Love is now filling up the air
I'm fully breathing it in
Laughing when people stare

This feeling is euphoric
And I'm happy for a change
I love it when the Lord takes notice
And seeks to rearrange

I am finally witnessing
What I thought I would never regain
It's such a lovely feeling
Knowing that love really does remain

Michelle Cook

Love Beyond a Shadow of a Doubt

I've loved you for as long as I can remember
Maybe even more
I'm still not sure how or when it began
But our love has endured
We've faced mountains of opposition
And still we continue to hold on
I have loved you beyond reason at times
Even feeling foolish for doing so
There were times when I questioned everything
I cannot forget how you tore my heart in two
Or how you decided to mend it all at once
The patching of it was quite painful
Like a threaded needle piercing my flesh
And yet I wanted you to do it
I figured how else could I ever live
I couldn't very well survive with a gaping wound
So I gave you a second chance
The opportunity to fix what was broken
There are days now
When I hardly even notice the scar
And yet others when it's still all I can see
You were the one person I could trust
The only one I had ever truly loved
But the inconceivable sins of life crushed us
Both of us were literally smashed into the ground
And normalcy hasn't been the same since

Perhaps this is progress right here
In these words and in the light of each new day
I'm discovering that I would rather die
Than to let you go from me
The shrapnel is still buried deep within my chest
A burden I will likely take to my grave
Yet I know I have no other choice
Because if I were to try and let you go
My soul would still cling to yours
The bond is too strong and the knot too tight
It's simply impossible to fully pull away
And so I'm trying desperately to let you back in
To trust you again the way I once did
And love you beyond a shadow of a doubt

Michelle Cook

From the Depths of My Heart

If you could read my thoughts
You would know how I feel

You would see the depths of my heart
And know my intentions are real

I think you would be
In complete disbelief

Yet a part of you would feel
Some sort of relief

You've only just been guessing
How deep my love goes

I think you'd be surprised
By what my heart really shows

To My Love, My Life

Can I really put into words
The way you make me feel
Each day I'm with you now
Seems almost unreal

I love you more
With every passing day
There's finally a closeness
Which had faded away

So many things
Tried to tear us apart
Never again my love
You have my whole heart

You and Me

Your smile brings me happiness
Your eyes make me blush
Your arms force me to slow down
When I find myself in a rush

Your words give me comfort
Your lap makes the perfect seat
Your lips ignite a passion
Before we drift off to sleep

Your laugh makes me feel giddy
Your touch seeks to thrill
Your mouth says you'll stay
And I believe you always will

Your soul seeks me out
Your embraces draw me near
Your body protects me
So I have nothing to fear

Your faith connects us
Your will has no end
Your devotion to me is something
In which I can always depend

Beneath the Canopy

Your gentleness soothes me
Your actions seek to convince my heart
Your kindness persuades me
And I think I'd feel lost if we were apart

Your affection has deepened
Your allegiance conveys the truth
Your love always feels authentic
And I yearn to spend a lifetime with you

Heart Issues

Fragile heart
Longing for passion
Attention starved
Seeking compassion

Willing heart
Craving more
Devotion neglected
Uncared for

Suffering heart
In need of repair
Unfulfilled dreams
Soul in despair

Aching heart
Yearning for affection
Easily forgotten
Tired of rejection

Fallen

I woke to find
The world remade
As I realized I'd fallen
For his sweet serenade
Now beneath the covers
Wrapped in pure bliss
Anxiously awaiting
Another gentle kiss

My Beloved

When I think of you
I know I will make it through

Whenever we're kept apart
A well of anguish consumes my heart

You're the one who lights the way
At the end of a long hard day

Only you beloved can make me feel complete
Without you here my life is bittersweet

I cannot even fathom not having you in my life
The pain I feel when you're away only brings me strife

Now that I've found you never let me go
Tell me that you'll always love me so

Constant Craving

Constantly craving
You by my side
In my heart
Is where you reside
Unfulfilled by
My current situation
My soul longs
For your reciprocation
This is how it is
Yet nothing can be done
So I'm missing out on a life
Full of so much fun
And if ever there was a way
To finally be free
I'd love you forever
Just you and me

I'll Always Love You

Cuddled under
A clouded sky
I glimpse a twinkle
In your eye

Staring back
I clearly see
Your sweet smile
Teasing me

Your warm hand
Pressed against mine
Our hearts beating
In rhythmic time

Your face is one
I'll never forget
Even when time
Has all been spent

Your love for me
Ever so true
It's why I promise
To always love you

Blanketed in Bliss

Warmth spread across her
As he gathered her in
And twilight awakened
His wickedly handsome grin
His devilish smirky smile
Sent shivers down her spine
And she squirmed underneath him
As he claimed her heart, soul, and mind

These are the Words

These are the words
That I wish I could say
To a man I once loved
Who drifted away

I loved you completely
And some days I still do
But something changed
And then you weren't you

The strings of my heart
Became twisted and frayed
I would have given anything
If you had just stayed

But time escaped
Never giving us a chance
Then love moved on
In search of romance

My broken heart seems
To hurt everyone I meet
Only jagged pieces remain
Most shattered at my feet

So I distance myself
Not wanting to pierce another
A life now spent alone
Without anyone to bother

A crushed spirit is all that's left
Just feel empty inside
Feels like the intricacies of me
Have all finally died

You Were Irresistible

You lightened my heart
Then blessed my soul

Always making me feel
Alive and whole

Why can't more people
Like you exist

It's why I could never
Find the will to resist

To Warm a Heart

Passionate kisses
Are the only way
To warm a heart
On a cold winters day

Cuddle close
Under a dim flicker of light
Lose yourself to love
Until everything's alright

Deepest Desires

She laid there beneath the satiny covers
Wishing to the ends of the earth she never had to leave
The feel of his strong arms around her
An inviting and warm comforting sleeve

The soothing sound of his beautiful heart
Beat rhythmically against her bare chest
She dared not even breathe
As his hands began to fondle and gently caress

The sensation was one she'd always dreamt of
And now her deepest desires were finally coming true
Her most sought-after wish was of him beside her
A blissful dream so long overdue

Caramel Kisses

Warm melty goodness
Takes me by surprise
As butterflies dance
In the light of your eyes

I swear I taste caramel
And you casually grin
Capturing my mouth
All over again

Fragile Whispers

His unexpected voice
Became a hushed affirmation
Murmuring softly
In the wee small hours of the night

An unforeseen dream
Full of promise and steadfast assurance
Undoubtedly she had heard it
His voice like a wish

So hauntingly beautiful
Was the far off isolated sound
The most fragile whisper
One could ever hear

She remembered the feel
Of the soft-spoken alluring words
As they pressed down gently
Upon her tortured soul

She yearned for more
Of the reverberating tone
Which had soothingly tugged
The strings of her heart

She lay there determined
Willing the words to resurface
A voice she would die for
Begging her dreams to carry her away

Empty Promises

Empty promises
Sealed their fate
He was gone
His chance too late

There were no words
To make it right
She finally saw him
In a different light

His tarnished heart
Would fool no more
Never again
Would she adore

Insincere actions
Created a veil
Causing their love
To finally derail

If only he'd kept
His promises to her
Their love would've lasted
Of this she's sure

Hints of Pleasure

Subtle hints
Sweetly spilled
A game we play
Leaves me thrilled
Tempting thoughts
Of what we could do
Giving pleasure
Just to you

I Never Really Believed

I never really believed in soul mates
Until the day I met him
There's just no good way to describe the feelings
That washed over me that day
A sudden warmth flooded my body
Every single time we would talk
Nothing seemed to make any sense
And yet everything was quite clear
I could feel his heart beating
In a distant place
He was so very far away
And yet my body could still sense his every move
The draw was magical and consumed me
To the brink of tears most days
For I could not see him, hold him, or touch him
And yet his mere existence wreaked havoc on my brain
The realization of him
Caused my life to spiral and spin out of control
I could no longer contain the emotions
Which were begging to rip my heart right out of my chest
And one day the sadness of a life without him
Became more than I could bear
So death finally had mercy upon my wearied soul
And saved me from a life which could never be

I Get Lost

I get lost in your eyes
Of burnished embers
Swept back in time
To happier Septembers
All of those autumn days
Have now passed us by
Time waits for no one
In a truth we can't deny

I Only Want You

It's been a whole year
Since I tried to say goodbye
I remember how brokenhearted you were
And how I made you cry

You made a heartfelt attempt
To become the man I needed
You did everything you could
Yet still I resisted as you pleaded

It's been a whole year
Since I tried to say goodbye
My heart was completely broken
And I no longer wanted to try

We faced a torrential storm
One I imagined we'd never get through
And during that difficult time
I pulled further away from you

It's been a whole year
Since I tried to say goodbye
I had come to the realization
That I couldn't forgive your lie

Beneath the Canopy

I tried in earnest
But my mind couldn't be erased
And every time I thought of us
I was left with a bitter taste

It's been a whole year
Since I tried to say goodbye
I wanted to let go
Even wished that I would die

But somehow love remained
Through those tormenting days
I began to see a different you
In your blue-eyed gaze

And now here we are
A thousand miles from each other
And I finally know for certain
That I'll never love another

For you have convinced me
Of your perfect love so true
And despite our painful past
I only want you

It Was the Seventh of June

It was the seventh of June
As she was walking by
And the way she moved
Had captured his eye

His soft feathery kiss
Floated by on the breeze
This unexpected peck
Made her weak in the knees

The brush of his lips
Against her skin so fair
Made her giggle and blush
As the wind tousled her hair

His sweet playful banter
Had initiated a connection
And her rosy red cheeks
Radiated love and affection

And time stood perfectly still
On that fateful afternoon
As two hearts collided
On that seventh of June

Illusionary Dreams

Merely an illusion
Sparked by a wish
Nothing was real
Just a fairytale kiss

Hopeless dreams
Floated endlessly by
Under an imagined
Sapphire blue sky

Pages left unwritten
Crumpled and set aside
The story unfinished
Her longing denied

Moonlight Reflections

Hazy
Her memories
Of a moonlight kiss.

Taken
From her mind
Did he even exist?

Empty
Her thoughts
Nothing seemed clear.

Futile
Those dreams
Hidden in a tear.

Just You and Me

Alone and free
Just you and me
Stone skipping
Skinny dipping
Freedom at last
Taking a chance
Finally living life
No more strife
Happy to be
Just you and me

Strawberry Kisses

Tempted by the taste
Of her strawberry kiss
The allurement of her
He just couldn't resist
One look into those eyes
Left him hungry for more
Always aching for her
To come and explore
The feel of her touch
Left him satisfied for days
And the more he had of her
The more he recklessly craved
There had never been another
Who pleased him like she did
If only the thrill of her
Wasn't wickedly forbid

Stubborn Truths

His reasons were abrupt and unclear
Rationale she could not discern
So she relinquished him from her heart
While he promised to never return
Months of anguish slipped on by
And the days grew cold and bleak
Both hearts in complete disrepair
Missing a love they vowed never to seek
A tragic story of stubborn truths
Would keep their troubled hearts at bay
Regrets filling their darkened skies
By what neither one would ever say

That Cold Winter Night

Quilted cotton sheets
Wrapped in cozy satisfaction
That cold winter night
Set the course of action

She gave him a look
From under those sheets
Sending his heart running
A thousand beats

He couldn't keep his eyes
From looking into hers
That night suddenly became
A full on blur

And the next morning came
All too soon
So they continued on
Throughout the afternoon

The Boy Who Read Her

With every emotion he could see right through
Always seeming to understand her every view
He could read her like an old familiar book
In every heartwarming and spellbinding look
His gaze always seemed to linger on her face
His thoughts and feelings she could almost taste
Connected in almost every possible way
To a boy she met by chance on a dull rainy day

The Embers Erupted

The embers erupted
Provoked once more
Our love had surely died
Then you reopened that door

You took me in your arms
Rekindling an exhausted flame
And our love grew stronger
As you staked your claim

In your sea colored eyes
I now see a passion so strong
And as you hold me in your arms
I know this is where I belong

We've been through so much
But I'm still holding on tight
For without you in my life
Things just wouldn't seem right

The Fire Raged

Beneath the surface
The fire raged
She his playmate
Now fully engaged
Each sensuous kiss
Fueled his desire
Leaving him feeling
Thoroughly inspired

Michelle Cook

Where the Raindrops Play

I'm forever trying to spend
As much time with you as I can
For neither of us really knows
When our lives here will come to an end
There might suddenly come a day
When you are taken far far away
Carried up into those majestic clouds
Where the raindrops seem to play
And if that very sad and terrible day
Should ever sorrowfully arrive
Promise me you'll send me showers
So that I know that you're still alive

This Life is too Short for Goodbyes

If my heart breaks hard enough
Will you be able to feel it?
I'm left standing here all alone
Sinking into the pit of despair
Wondering how I will ever survive
Our souls have just been ripped apart
Mine bleeding the very instant you drove away
And I'll never forget your face
Downcast and regretful
This life too short for goodbyes

You're Everything to Me

You've loved me more
Than a thousand oceans ever could

You've stood by my side
Through the fiercest of storms

You've stayed with me
Even as the waves pummeled your chest

You've shown me how much you care
With every soothing word you've whispered

You've been the anchor of my soul
And the healer of my heart

You've been the world to me
Even during my darkest days

You've shown me just how easily
Love can stand the test of time

You've been my firm foundation
And the rock on which I stand

You're everything to me
Because He is everything to you

It's that kind of love which sets you apart
And makes me love you even more

To Kiss a Rainbow

Stabbed by one last
Poisoned remark
Left her spiraling
Into a realm of dark

Reaching up
She captured a cloud
Darkened it was
By a looming shroud

Shaking out
The murky matter
She caught her breath
As the sky did shatter

Then spotting a rainbow
She grabbed on tight
Kissing and hugging it
With all of her might

Ties

These ties
They tug
Against
My failing heart

A permanent
Reminder
That we
Are connected

Neither space
Nor time
Can erase
You

This is simply
The way
It is
Now and forevermore

Brokenness Defined

Every beat of your enticing heart
Mesmerized and controlled my spirit
Bound by your enchantments
Your invisible barricade eluded me

Hovering unbeknownst by day
Drifting aimlessly by night

The sting of unrequited love
Tormented my very being
Emptying my soul of emotion
Yet I couldn't say goodbye

Every ounce of me loved you
With an incredible fierceness

Reaching far beyond the dimensions
Of an ordinary human heart
It was only after you pierced my soul
With the truth of an unforgivable indiscretion
That my spirit could no longer see clearly

Beneath the Canopy

Clinging to the scraps of your essence
I had no other alternative but to let you go
My lifeblood now begged to intermingle
With someone who had an honorable disposition

This was the last thought I incurred
Before completely breaking free

Heartbroken I left for another realm
Where love seemed entirely possible
A place where hope seemed to dwell
And you became a fragmented memory
Too sharp to handle anymore

Michelle Cook

Brokenness Rescinded

Your unavoidable eyes
A sea of cerulean blue and grey
Beckon me lovingly
Back into promise filled arms

My shattered heart
Desperately trying to mend
A thousand broken pieces
Scattered among blood stained sheets

Lost in rose-colored dreams
I lose myself in a wave of forgiveness
Saturated by your enthusiasm
Consumed by your renewed vigor

I yearn for what you are willing to offer
Craving the love which you've unburied

Still remaining unquestionably hesitant
Yet finally stripped of the barriers
Which had grown to impossible heights

Beneath the Canopy

Your love is now evident on every level
And has stolen away my shaken breath

Forcing my eyes to witness a miracle
You have now become my reality
An impossible prism filled vision

Fulfilled in the wake of a calamitous ordeal
A love ever so gently rekindled and reborn
From the sorrows of a duplicitous life

Unwavering in earnestness
Wholly mending an irreparable heart

Is it Real?

Kissing you still causes a tingling sensation
Which travels all the way down to my toes
Leaves me feeling blissfully happy
Always yearning for more as you know

After all these years do you feel it too
The euphoria of such an intimate act
Or have you grown accustomed to my touch
And feel like you can no longer react

I never grow tired of what we have
Or how amazingly good you make me feel
But sometimes I wonder if it's all just an act
Or if your love for me is truly real

Even though we've been together forever
I know how tiresome some years have been
And along the way we've had so many times
When we've kind of had to start again

So tell me do you really love me
Like you promised you always would
I want us both to love each other
The way we really should

The Last Thread

One last thread
Given by him
Deeply woven
Completely hid

A golden thread
Hard to break
A gleaming reminder
Of what's at stake

Knotted and tied
Constricting her heart
Leaving her writhing
From the very start

Never to Love Again

I feel deep in my heart
That I shall never love again
Seems too late in life
For something more to begin
I really never expected
To fall out of love
This was just one of those things
I had never thought of
So now that it's happened
I'm unsure of what to do
It seems this emptiness in my heart
Nothing can undo
I have everything I could ever want
And so much more
So why am I giving up the one
I used to love and adore

Abandoned Hearts

Drawn to each other
By a magnetic force
Their ephemeral love blossomed
And ran its course
Eventually indecision came
Leaving abandoned hearts
Under a shattered sky
No hope for the future
Two young lovers said goodbye
With ambitions and dreams
Each moved on
Never speaking again
Their love now gone

Distract Me

Distract me with your kisses
Anything to eliminate this surging pain
I'm in need of your gentle caresses
So I don't completely go insane

Give me something else to focus on
Send me to a place far away from here
Won't you please distract all of my senses
So I'm not driven mad with tears

Save me from myself
And rid my body of this misery
Distract me with your everlasting love
So I can be set free

Distract me with your warm embrace
It's the only thing that really works
Unhinge me with your love
And take away everything that hurts

Young Love

Take me back in time
When our love was very new
All I want is you

A True Cord of Love

The filaments of affection
Are often broken
Tossed to the side
Like an old forgotten token
Sometimes a thread of devotion
Just cannot stay
It's the truth I'm afraid
Though it's sad to say
And some strands are merely
Carried away on the breeze
Eventually settling in
Somewhere amongst the trees
Yet a true cord of love
Is hardly ever lost
For losing one of these
Comes with an insurmountable cost

You... Summed Up in Seven Words

Warm breath on cool skin
Tender lips lovingly explore
Strong hands caress
Seeking fingers tempt
Playful kisses arouse
Gentle bites stimulate
Inviting tongue tantalizes

Is There Someone?

Is there someone you cannot forget?
A person you loved deeply without regret.

Is there somebody who still lingers in your heart?
They always have from the very start.

Is there a sense that this person is ever near?
A lovely face smiling in a distant mirror.

Is there a longing which just won't relent?
When you remember the days you often spent.

Is there a way to go on and forget those years?
Without finding yourself crying a million tears.

Is there any way to completely move on?
When you dream of them every day from dusk until dawn.

Is there a cure for a saddened soul?
When life has surely taken its toll.

Is there a way to recover from despair?
When the person that caused it isn't even aware.

Fleeting Moments of Love

Love burned a hole
Right through her heart

Hidden under the ashes
A few embers still remain

An occasional fire erupts
Igniting a momentary flame

Extinguished by nothing more
Than a slight passing breeze

Michelle Cook

Love Isn't for the Fainthearted

All I could think of
Were depressive thoughts
My stomach was completely
Tied up in knots
I hadn't eaten anything
In a zillion days
I laid there on my bed
In complete malaise
The absence of him
Was more than I could bear
All I could do
Was lay there and stare
My body felt heavy
I just couldn't move
I knew that without him
I would never improve
The minutes felt like days
And the days felt like years
And I found myself crying
An insane amount of tears
The earth completely shattered
On the day he departed
I now realize that love
Isn't for the fainthearted

Love is All That Truly Matters

Love is still loving somebody
Even when that someone doesn't love you back

Love is forgiving somebody
Even when it seems hopelessly impossible

Love is putting someone else first
Even when it seems entirely unfair

Love is still caring for somebody
Even after being hurt by them

Love is looking for the good in someone's heart
Even when the exterior seems unlovable

Love is showing kindness to somebody
Even when that same compassion isn't returned

Love is the only word which has ever truly mattered
And the only word which ever truly will

Beloved

Be mine forevermore
May our love be everlasting and eternally soar

Eagerly I wait
My only hope is that you will not hesitate

Longing everyday only for you
I know these feelings are honest and true

Only God knows what the future holds
But a love like this could never grow old

Verily I am sure
That our love will now and forever endure

Everything I envision
Secures any sort of doubt or indecision

Delay my heart no more
It is you that I will forever adore

Do You Know?

Do you know what you mean to me,
Can you feel my love clinging to your heart?

Do I remind you enough each and every day,
Of how much I've cared for you from the start?

Can you see the sparkle in my eyes,
The way I light up when you are near.

Do you fully understand this depth of love,
Have I made myself perfectly clear?

Do you realize how much you amaze me,
By the things you say and do.

Well if it isn't completely obvious yet,
Here's your reminder that *I Love You!*

Oh... Happiness

Oh the pleasure of happiness
Cannot easily be defined
It's a feeling you often get
When someone is very kind

It can leave you feeling giddy
Inattentive and unaware
Because you're so filled with wonder
It often makes people stare

The excitement you're flooded with
Is often a rare occurrence
Which makes a person hopeful
For an everyday reassurance

Happiness for me
Is a state of satisfaction
Which causes a distinct smile
As an immediate reaction

It often takes a bit of time
To find happiness where you are
And yet when it finally comes
It can be strikingly bizarre

Beneath the Canopy

I still have yet to define
Such an extraordinary word
And the feelings that it brings
Can be quite absurd

I am however quite convinced
Of at least one thing
That love can fully be captured
By what true happiness can bring

Passionate

Pulling you close
I feel your beating heart
Anticipation floods my soul
And I'm eager to start
Shivering next to you
Warmth is what I seek
Shaken by your fiery kisses
I'm unable to speak
Ignited by the warmth
Of your soothing touch
Overwhelmed by desire
I want you so much
Never ending ecstasy
Wreaks havoc on my brain
Alluring sensations
Let us never again refrain
Tantalizing caresses
Fuel the flames of passion
Enraptured by you
Inextinguishable attraction

The Way of Love

I've confessed so many things
Not a single heartfelt word reciprocated
But isn't that the way of love
We can give our whole heart away
And never receive even a sliver in return
And when the day finally comes
When this life is done and I am gone
I will have given everything I've got
Loved as hard and painfully as I can
And I'll know that it was all worth it
Because to love without being loved
Is the greatest gift anybody can ever give

Love

Love is a spontaneous thing
It often follows a dance in the rain
Love cannot be understood
The feeling of its presence overwhelms as it should
Love is a special reminder
Of God's grace as our provider
Love cannot be mistaken
The heart will always feel as if it's been shaken
Love is a light that grows brighter each day
It even shines in the night when there's nothing left to say
Love of a true kind cannot be broken
The emotions it creates are overwhelming and unspoken
Love is a mysterious wonder
Careful… or it will pull you under

Free Love

It's hard to give my love away
And not receive it in return
I wonder if this heart of mine
Will ever really learn

ABOUT THE AUTHOR

Michelle Cook resides in Wisconsin with her husband and two youngest daughters. She is the author of a historical fiction book; Revelations of the Past, which can be found at; www.channillo.com.

Originally from California, Michelle joined the Army after graduating high school and worked as an Intelligence Analyst. While in the military, she married and started her family. After her time in the military, she moved to Wisconsin and worked in the Biotechnology field.

Michelle is currently a full-time writer/blogger and homeschooling mother. In her free time, she can be found traveling to remote places and finds the majority of her creative inspiration during her great outdoor adventures.

To find out more about Michelle Cook, visit her website at; www.herwritinghaven.com.

www.ingramcontent.com/pod-product-compliance
Lightning Source LLC
Chambersburg PA
CBHW032358040426
42451CB00006B/53